Fire! Fi

*Written by Barrie Wade and Maggie Moore
Illustrated by Bethan Matthews*

Contents

Chapter 1   **The New Roof**   4

Chapter 2   **The Drama**   15

Chapter 3   **School's Burning!**   25

Chapter 1
The New Roof

Mrs Smart was in a dangerous mood.

The morning had been bad enough, but now, as she marked the afternoon register, she was clearly at the end of her tether.

"Kim," she called tersely.

A furious bout of hammering outside drowned Kim's reply.

"Kim," she called again crossly.

Again the hammering drowned Kim's answer.

"Kim Luk, will you wake up, please!" cried Mrs Smart.

"I am awake, Mrs Smart. I did… "

The rest of Kim's words were again drowned by hammering, but it was enough for Mrs Smart to realise what had happened.

"I'm sorry, Kim," Mrs Smart said. "Pete."

"Yes, Mrs Smart," yelled Pete, just as the hammering suddenly stopped. His voice screeched in the silence.

Everyone jumped, then laughed.

"There's no need to shout, Pete."

"I'm sorry," said Pete. "I thought you couldn't hear."

"Well, I'm not deaf," said Mrs Smart, "though I soon will be. How I am expected to teach under these conditions I do not know."

She looked out of the window; so did everyone else.

Clouds of smoke were billowing from a tar boiler close to Mr Baker's classroom. The roof repairers were laying new roofing felt and spreading tar on it. Again the hammering started as they fixed more felt.

Mr Baker's classroom was empty. That may have made the banging sound louder. It sounded as if a huge drum was being struck by hammers.

Mrs Treadgold had made the announcement about the new roof in assembly three weeks ago.

"Workers will soon be here to repair the roof of Mr Baker's classroom," she had said. "All Mr Baker's class will have a letter to take home to their parents. They will have to stay at home for the last week of term."

All Mr Baker's class had cheered.

"Hush!" Mrs Treadgold had said, smiling, "but Mr Baker will still be in school as usual." Everyone had looked at Mr Baker who had pulled a face.

Now the hammering suddenly stopped.

"I wish *we* could have had the week off," said David.

"So do I," said Mrs Smart with some feeling. "But it's not for me to say. You all have to stay and work hard for your test in May."

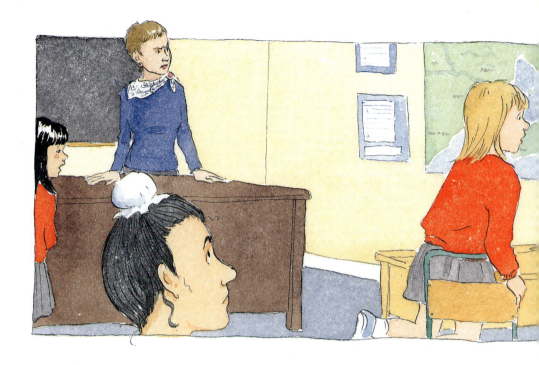

"It's not fair," said Sally. "Mr Baker's class has an extra week of holiday."

"But they don't have tests to do next term and it's their roof that is leaking," said Mrs Smart.

She seemed to have forgotten the register. "Why they can't do these jobs in the Easter holiday I don't know! It is impossible to... "

Another bout of hammering drowned the rest of her words and a cloud of smoke from the tar boiler billowed their way.

"It really stinks, Miss," said Sally, when the hammering stopped.

"Well, move your chair away from the window, then," said Mrs Smart kindly. "I think we'll just have a quiet afternoon without lessons."

"It won't be very quiet, Mrs Smart," said Kim.

"No, I don't suppose it will." Mrs Smart smiled briefly, but her smile was driven away again by the hammers.

A roofer passed by the window and grinned. Mrs Smart glared at him.

"Can we have a quiz, Miss?" asked Ben.

"No, I don't think so," replied Mrs Smart.

"Oh, please, Miss!"

"Can we do drama?" asked Anna.

"Yes! Yes, please," cried several voices.

Mrs Smart paused. Everyone could see that they had won.

"Why not?" Mrs Smart said briskly, her eyes twinkling. "I don't care if it's not in the curriculum. This smoke gives me an idea. We *will* do drama. How about the Great Fire of London?"

Everyone cheered.

Chapter 2
The Drama

Mrs Smart smiled again briefly. Then, in between the banging, she described London at the time of the Plague. She told the class about the filthy, narrow streets, the rats, and the many wooden houses that were so close together.

Then she told how the fire started in Pudding Lane. Some people believed it was started in the shop of a careless French pastry cook. Once it had started, the strong wind fanned the flames and the fire spread rapidly. The hand pumps were useless against the massive fire. People plunged into the river to escape and even blew up houses with gunpowder to try to stop the inferno.

"Now," said Mrs Smart when she had finished, "work in four groups and prepare a short play. You don't have to write anything down unless you want to."

Pete and Kulbir, Ben and David formed Group One with Sally and Rachel, Kim and Anna. They decided to write down their drama script. All the groups soon had their plays prepared. It was easier to work through the hammering because each group stayed close together. Finally the noise stopped altogether as the roofers came down from their work for a tea break. Their tar boiler flickered and smelly smoke still swirled in the wind, but at least it was quieter.

Group One was the first to perform its play for the rest of the class. They only had one copy of the drama script, so they gave it to Mrs Smart.

London on Fire

Cast (in order of appearance)

Town Crier	Anna
French Pastry Cook	Kim
Lord Mayor of London	David
Chief of Police	Ben
Citizen 1	Pete
Citizen 2	Kulbir
Lord Mayor's Wife	Sally
Citizen 3	Rachel

Town Crier	London's burning!
French Pastry Cook	London's burning!
Lord Mayor of London	Fetch the engine!
Chief of Police	Fetch the engine!
Citizen 1	Fire! Fire!
Citizen 2	Fire! Fire!
Lord Mayor's Wife	Pour on water!
Citizen 3	Pour on water!

Town Crier	Oyez! Oyez! Pray silence for his Worship the Lord Mayor of London.
Citizen 1	*(to the Lord Mayor)* What are you going to do to save our homes?
Citizen 2	*(to the Lord Mayor)* You had better do something!
Citizen 3	*(to the Lord Mayor)* The fire is getting nearer.

Town Crier	Well, be quiet and listen to what the Lord Mayor has to say.
Lord Mayor	Thank you. Now we have a big problem. We can't stop the fire with buckets of water.
Lord Mayor's Wife	We'll have to go and jump in the river, but I can't swim.
Lord Mayor	Never mind about that.

(Enter Chief of Police with French Pastry Cook, carrying a mixing bowl.)

Chief of Police	Your Worship, I have caught the one who started the fire.
Citizens	Boo! Throw him in the river!
Town Crier	Hush!
Lord Mayor	Well, what have you got to say?
French Pastry Cook	It wasn't my fault. Maybe the tarts caught fire. They went up in smoke.
Citizen 1	So have the houses.

Citizen 2	So have the churches.
Citizen 3	So have the inns.
Citizen 1	It's his fault.
Citizen 2	Yes, he's to blame.
Citizen 3	Throw him in the river.
Lord Mayor's Wife	Oh dear, can he swim?
Lord Mayor	Stop this nonsense. We must stop the fire. Has anybody any ideas?
Chief of Police	Yes, your Worship. The houses are too close together. If we can get rid of some houses, we can stop the fire spreading.
Lord Mayor	How can we get rid of houses? How can we do that?
Chief of Police	With gunpowder. We'll blow them up.
Lord Mayor's Wife	What a clever idea.
Lord Mayor	Right, start with those three houses over there.

Citizen 1 ⎫	*speaking*	You can't do that!
Citizen 2 ⎬	*at the*	That's where I live!
Citizen 3 ⎭	*same time*	That's my house!

Lord Mayor — We have to do it.
(to Chief of Police) Blow them up quickly. The fire is getting nearer.

Chief of Police — Yes, your Worship. At once, your Worship.

Lord Mayor's Wife — Quickly! There's no time to lose!

Town Crier — London's burning!

French Pastry Cook — London's...

"Fire! Fire!" yelled Ben.

"Not yet!" said David. "We say 'Fetch the engine' first."

"No! Fire! Look! Real fire, I mean," yelled Ben again. He pointed at the window.

Chapter 3
School's Burning!

As Ben pointed at the window, everyone turned to look. The smoke was now blacker and denser. There were flames flickering on the flat roof of Mr Baker's classroom and also from the wood around the window. Flames from the tar boiler licked against the woodwork.

"Look, Mrs Smart, the school's on fire."

"Right, everybody," said Mrs Smart quietly. "Stand up. Walk out quickly and quietly and stand in the playground. You know the drill. Leave your things here."

Mrs Smart set off the fire alarm, picked up the register and followed everyone out. She calmly closed the door.

In the playground she called the register. As everyone answered their names, their eyes were on the flames dancing on the flat roof and climbing up the wall near the boiler. Workers were shouting and running about, but they didn't seem to know what to do.

Mrs Smart finished the register and said briskly, "Good, that's everyone."

"Longdale's burning, Longdale's burning," Ben sang.

"That will do, Ben," said Mrs Smart firmly, but she didn't look cross.

"We could blow up our classroom to stop the fire spreading," said Sally. All the class laughed.

"It didn't work in the Great Fire, so I don't think it will work here, Sally," Mrs Smart said with a smile.

Then they heard the fire engine.

"Good," said Mrs Smart. "Stand right back against the wall." The roofers stood about looking sheepish.

"Well, children, you can see how too many careless cooks spoil the pastry," said Mrs Smart.

Everybody laughed again.

"That's good, Miss," said Kim.

The roofers looked puzzled.

Then the fire engine drove into the playground and the firefighters jumped out. They unwound a hose and began to spray water on the fire.

"I didn't know the Fire Brigade carried water with them," said Kulbir.

"Yes," said Anna. "It saves lots of time."

"They could have done with that in the Great Fire of London," said Rachel. "They only had hand pumps."

It took only a few seconds for the flames to disappear in a hiss of steam. The smoke lessened too. Then two firefighters climbed up to the roof and sprayed water up and down on the new felt that was still smoking. Very soon it was all over.

Mrs Treadgold came over to talk to the class. She told all the class she was proud of them and how grown up they had acted by walking calmly and quietly out of the classroom. Mrs Smart smiled.

"It looks as if all the roofing work will have to be started again," Mrs Treadgold told them.

"Oh, no!" groaned Kulbir. Mrs Smart looked grim.

"But," Mrs Treadgold went on, "this class has suffered enough. You can all stay at home and have the rest of the week away from school."

"Hurray!" cried Ben.

Everybody cheered.

"But remember, you must practise for your tests next term. Mrs Smart will set you some work to do over Easter."

However, nobody minded that.

The firefighters let everybody try on their tall yellow helmets and, before they left, all the class had a look inside the fire engine.

"I'm going to be a firefighter when I grow up," said Pete.

"Me too," said Anna. "You can really help people in a job like that."

"You might learn about a very famous fire next year in your new school," said Mrs Treadgold. "The Great Fire of London."

"Oh, we know all about that," said Sally. "It started in Pudding Lane."

"Yes, it was carelessness that started it there, like here," said Kulbir.

"People accused a French pastry cook," said Pete.

"And the houses caught fire quickly because they were made of wood," said Anna.

"The wind fanned the flames," said Kim.

"So the Lord Mayor had some houses blown up with gunpowder to stop the fire," said Ben.

"But it didn't work," added David.

"At least it got rid of the Plague," said Rachel.

Mrs Treadgold looked surprised, but also pleased. "Well, if you can remember facts so well, you won't have any problems with your tests after Easter," she said. "Well done, everybody. Now get your coats and get ready for home."

She turned to Mrs Smart and said, "You have some bright sparks in your class."

"And I'm not going to pour cold water on them," said Mrs Smart.

Both teachers laughed.

Everyone was pleased to see Mrs Smart looking happy again.

As they went home, she was trying on a firefighter's helmet.